forest whispers

forest whispers

retreat in
nature

Natalie Cooper
Sonia Wynn-Jones (MBRCP)

———

Foreword by
Professor Sir Cary L. Cooper, CBE

Contents

——

Foreword
Preface
Introduction
Message from Sonia Wynn-Jones
Silent meditation & guidance

1. Journeying – Spiritual awakening

- I am a maiden voyage
- Turn with a different tide
- Pearl in the sand

2. Grief & forgiveness – Moving forward

- Empowerment
- Gift of forgiveness

3. Inner strength – Self-esteem

- Spider's web
- Inner violin
- Cycle of self-realisation

4. Guided wisdom – Clarity of thought

- The sliver moonlight stag
- Wand of life

5. Charms of protection – Understanding our light

- Light
- White feathers

6. Realise your dreams – Letting go

- Your field of dreams awaits you…
- Authentic pathway
- A wishing well

7. Self-awareness – Strengthening ourselves

- Silver birch
- Safe passage
- Follow the breath of your kite

8. Follow your rainbow – Overcoming fear

- A heart of roses
- Buttercups
- Gold-dust

9. Insight & vision – Enlightenment

- Shoal of gifts
- Majestic wings
- Liberation

10. Pained relationships – Acceptance

- Pools of love
- Tortured love
- Passing of light

11. Lovers' merriment – Attracting love

- Floating atom
- I want to dance in your eyes
- Pair of doves

12. Loving relationships – Unconditional love

- Hearth and home
- Guardian angel
- Raptures of a fair kiss

About the authors
Acknowledgements
Photo credits

Foreword

———

Many of us lead frenetic lives, symbolized by mobiles seemingly attached to our ears most of the day. We are constantly connected to emails, mobiles and social media. We never have any 'reflection time', time to be by ourselves to reflect on our life and what we want to achieve in life.

'Time out' is important for all of us but we rarely achieve it. Instead, we're constantly running on the proverbial life's treadmill all the time.

Work-life balance is one of the great challenges of today's world, with two out of every three families now dual earners. Long working hours, the lack of flexible working and the multiple demands of work and family have led to unprecedented stress on working parents, as they juggle conflicting pressures. Flexible working is one such solution.

In seeking to improve the quality of working life, 'work-life balance', recent years have seen the focus shift from workplace 'stress' to workplace 'wellbeing' – in other words, creating environments where employees can enjoy a good quality of life while at work. This has been my challenge ever since I was a social worker in a deprived part of the city of Los Angeles when doing my MBA, something I will never forget and stays with me 50 years on.

I witnessed great deprivation in LA. But I also watched people on the edge of existence grow in resilience as a result of the patience, kindness and care of the skilled and compassionate social workers dedicated to helping them.

All of us can make a difference to others' lives by listening and being there for them.

Since the financial crisis of 2008, most organisations have reduced their staff numbers, to keep labour costs down. This has left their remaining employees overloaded, working longer hours, feeling less job secure and under increased micro-management by their line manager, as pressure mounts from above on bottom line delivery. It's a perfect storm for workplace stress.

In the UK, recession and job insecurity has intensified even further under the cloud of Brexit. When we feel uncertain, we are likely to resist change and stay put – even in a dysfunctional work environment. We need to feel secure, valued and trusted to embrace change and accept new challenges within our current organisations or elsewhere.

We need humane leadership at all levels of our organisations – people who will treat others with compassion and care, relating to them as they would like their children's employers to treat his or her children.

Being in touch with our feelings is critical if we want to achieve a modicum of happiness and inner peace, but only a few of us ever do this. Knowing ourselves is essential for human growth, and, as the saying goes: "If you always do what you always did, you'll always get what you always got."

Each of us needs to ignore the nay-sayers, 'glass have empty types' who fill the world with negative energy, and work with positive and supportive people who embrace making necessary changes in work or in life generally.

When you come across people who are consistently 'glass half empty', don't try to change them, find others who are 'glass nearly full'. Positive and supportive people will help you grow. As Mark Twain wrote: "Keep away from people who try to belittle your ambitions. Small people always do that, but the really great make you feel that you, too, can somehow become great."

It is about taking control of your life. As the playwright George Bernard Shaw wrote in his play 'Mrs. Warren's Profession': "People are always blaming their circumstances for what they are. I don't believe in circumstances. The people who get on in this world are the people who get up and look for the circumstances they want, and if they can't find them, make them!".

—————

Professor Sir Cary L. Cooper, CBE

50th Anniversary Professor of Organizational Psychology & Health, Manchester Business School, University of Manchester, President of CIPD, President of the British Academy of Management, President of Relate, President of the Institute of Welfare

Preface

_____

*Throughout life we've all
been on many journeys and
experienced a whole spectrum
of varying emotions.*

Our lives are continuous stories, made
up of different chapters. We don't
know the ending until one chapter
closes and another one opens.

Some chapters in our lives may
contain endless suffering, pain and
trauma, while others are blissful,
wondrous and magical.

Messages of hope

———

When stories are translated into meaningful messages, they can move us to tears or make our hearts sing with joy. We can find solace, peace or comfort by taking in a few chosen words or passages that strike a powerful chord within us.

Stories can contain a wealth of spiritual messages and symbolism that resonate with us on a deeply personal level. Sometimes, the messages we receive are a timely reminder that we can change our destiny and it's within our own control to turn our lives around.

Other peoples' life events, current
or historic, can be motivational:

- Stories can give us the courage
  to take a risk or a step forward

- Stories can charge our emotions
  and change our thoughts in
  a heartbeat

- Stories have the power to be life
  changing and liberating

Journeys of survival –
we are never alone

The adage: 'you're not on your own'
has never rung more true for me.
We are never alone.

Even in the depths of despair, looking into a darkened black vat, we are never alone. When we feel the world is against us and we're truly on the edge, we always have our inner voice. If we listen hard to it, it will tell us that we can get through the bleakness. For it is only temporary.

We can visualise getting through to the other side, coming out of a black, winding tunnel. No matter how long we have to walk through it without light, once we see even a small glimmer, we know we can survive the journey and go on to win in life.

Every experience, no matter how hard, is a lesson that tests us, builds our strength of character and makes us more resilient. In fact, there are many reasons for the challenges that confront us in life, even to the point of changing our life's path.

Keeping the faith

––––––

When we have faith, there is hope.
Keeping it is challenging but even
when we lose it briefly, something will
present itself in an unexpected guise
to help us regain that faith. It could
be a message from a friend or the
kindness from a total stranger who
offers us help when we're in need.

Sometimes, we receive spiritual
guidance. We may not even recognise
it at the time, but at some point we will
realise that we were being given signs
and symbols.

Introduction

———

Writing, storytelling, travel and connecting with people from all walks of life is second nature to me.

In 2003 I embarked on a life changing, 'round-the-world' trip for nine months. Together with a very dear friend from my school days, I journeyed on and off the beaten tracks of China, Hong Kong, Thailand, Cambodia, Vietnam, Australia, New Zealand, Chile, Argentina, Bolivia, Peru and Brazil. We shared a camera, capturing scenes and moments that moved us or caught our eye.

A few years later, I've found they illustrate my personal, spiritual journey. Along with photos I've taken of nature, flowers and animals during my walking retreats.

forest whispers *is based on my*
personal journeys.

It is a set of powerful visualisations
written in the form of poetry and
prose that came from a higher place
of consciousness.

Since I was a small child, the
woodland has come to symbolise my
inner sanctuary. It is a safe place to
where I can retreat, under the canopy
of trees, surrounded by wild flowers,
trickling streams and the playful
innocence of woodland creatures.

By retreating into nature, I always find peace, love and harmony. Nature restores balance, provides clarity and fresh perspective.

When I need to escape the rigours of life, I seek the solitude of the forest. For if you listen, you can hear it whisper to you. I always leave the forest with a smile and secret told.

Using creativity as freedom to express and self-reflect my inner thoughts and feelings over my lifetime has offered me comfort, guidance and hope. It has got me through the dark days and also helped me to celebrate life.

The guidance I have unknowingly received during my journey through life has been a source of inspiration – giving me courage to realise my dreams, be true to myself and let go of past pain and bitterness. It has been about finding the ability to forgive, not necessarily to forget, and discovering the path that has led me to new beginnings and opportunities.

When I write, take photos or draw, I get wrapped up in a feeling of pure artistic magic in which I am able to surrender to my innermost intuition. I feel as though an electric current is running through me. This energy fuels my creativity and takes me on an unexpected journey.

My writing, especially, has provided an emotional outlet and been a huge part of my healing process. The creative spirit that had been present in me as a child sprang back to life.

In 2004, I reached a crisis point that triggered an emotional and spiritual awakening within me.

As I wrote the poems that now form the bedrock of this book, I realised that words of wisdom, from I knew not where, were pouring out onto the pages and I started to understand that my childhood dreams of being a creative writer might well come to fruition. Having been on a healing journey, and in a period of transition for many years, I have been reunited with my childhood talents.

I've sought out and been blessed to have met some wonderful, caring, loving, healing counsellors and spiritual mentors who have assisted me with guidance. With this support and encouragement, I am now able to 'stand alone' with self-belief.

Most importantly, I cannot thank enough my meditation teacher, mentor and spiritual guide, Sonia Wynn-Jones. Sonia has provided me with the reflective space I needed in order to heal myself and she continues to do so. She introduced me to the greatest gift of all – meditation.

I met Sonia around 15 years ago. I belong to her weekly meditation and monthly spiritual and personal development group. She is an incredible healer and intuitive guidance counsellor. I now practice silent meditation on a daily basis. Through Sonia, I have come to understand my spiritual journey, which in turn has awakened my sense of purpose.

It's all about the timing and the lessons that have to be learnt along the way before you can begin to make your dream a reality.

This book is about sharing those lessons, sharing love, and hopefully helping others to get on the road to enlightenment.

A message from Sonia Wynn-Jones, MBRCP

─────

Spiritualism gives you what you need. The truth.

Meditation is the tool that enables your mind to quieten sufficiently, to allow expansion and growth at soul level.

People have such strength buried deep inside them. They just have to learn to tap into it through the quietening of silent meditation.

Life slings all kinds of rubbish at us. We can't change that, but through the quietening of meditation we can stop ourselves from knee-jerk reacting. We are able to take a breath and tap into the quiet, and handle whatever we come across in a far more measured way.

Things happen for a reason, they just do. There's no point being angry or scared. You can turn your experiences into something positive and focus on that, instead of being seduced by the negative.

Silent meditation
& guidance

———

What is meditation?

———

Meditation is a profound quietening of the monkey mind, including the endless 'to do' lists and the constant conversations in our minds. We quieten to such a degree that we are able to surrender into a different dimension of consciousness.

It's learning to push back our over-busy, over-analytical mind. By meditating, you allow headspace for clarity of thought and heightened intuition.

When people meditate for the first time, they have no idea what to expect or what they might experience. They tend to think that meditating is for relaxation alone.

In fact, it is so much more than that and there are many forms of meditation such as transcendental, Buddhist, yogic and guided meditation. Personally I practice silent meditation, though any form of meditation is better than none.

Why meditate?

——

Meditation has been with us for many thousands of years. For Buddhist monks, meditation started as a form of prayer. While it remains a form of prayer, it has developed into something that helps us manage the frenetic everyday lives we lead in today's world.

Meditation transcends all religions yet conflicts with none of them. It stops us surrendering to the negatives in our lives and helps us harness positive energies.

Meditation can help us heal and nurture our minds and our bodies. If we have an illness that is long-term or for which there is no cure, meditation will not necessarily cure us. However, it will heal the mind, allowing us to accept our situation and therefore reduce the effects of the disease. Meditation brings in a positive mind, positive thinking, and positive energy. This can only be beneficial to help us overcome and diminish pain.

Self-nurture

We have to take that time out for
ourselves. Self-nurturing comes first
before anything. I can't begin to stress
strongly enough the importance of
self-nurturing.

If we are not in the right place physically and mentally, we cannot help or heal ourselves, let alone anyone else.

Self-nurture seems like an indulgence to us. There are so many things at our fingertips to help us self-nurture. However for many, it still feels embarrassing to show anyone else or even admit to ourselves that we might need help. Sadly this is a human trait, it's part of the way we are wired and not very helpful.

Today, mental health issues have less of a stigma than ever before. We also know how to take care of our bodies. We have so much personal choice, it's now commonplace, almost social, to go the gym, go for a walk, run or a bike ride. For many of us, it wasn't always this way.

Getting a grasp on self-nurturing is a challenge and the majority of people don't want to ask for help. This is pure ego.

Avoiding burn out

———

None of us want to be seen in need.
It's part of the human condition. It's
pride. We have to understand why we
have pride. Pride is based on ego. We
do not want to be crumbling, needy
or weak. This is not essentially a bad
thing as it can help us to self-govern
our emotions. Yet, when it becomes
evident that nothing you have tried
is solving your issue, you have a right
and need to seek help.

Life has progressed to such a degree
and everything is so fast. Fast
technology. Fast transport. We don't
have time any more to ponder things.
We don't think before we write or
speak. There is no time!

The speed with which we live our lives isn't always bad, but to manage our lives we need some respite and this is offered to us in the form of meditation. It keeps us grounded and on an even keel, sufficiently quietened to keep up with the speed of everyday life. Yes I do mean *quietened*. This in no way slows us down. It just enables us to cope with our over-busy lives more efficiently and without 'burning out'.

Benefits of meditation

———

Many recent studies have shown that while meditation is greatly relaxing and provides us with a sense of wellbeing, there are also many spiritual, emotional and physical benefits. It actually affects the part of your brain that regulates positive emotions.

It has also been shown that people who meditate experience an increase in 'whole brain thinking and learning'. This provides greater mental clarity, which creates more efficiency.

Those of us who practice daily meditation don't need scientific validation of the benefits, but it does at least validate what has been claimed by the most enlightened of spiritual masters and practitioners for thousands of years.

Benefits of meditation

___

Physically:

- Lower heart rate
- Lower stress levels
- Lower anxiety levels
- Decrease in high blood pressure
- Lowering of cholesterol levels
- Reduced risk of cardiovascular disease
- Improved breathing which can aid asthma sufferers
- Can improve conditions such as allergies and arthritis

Emotionally:

- Improved thought processes
- Increased creativity
- Relief from depression
- Decreased mood swings
- Improved memory
- Raised self-awareness
- Higher energy levels
- Increased positivity
- Emotional stability

Spiritually:

- Heightened intuition
- Greater self-awareness
- Creates a sense of unconditional love and self-value
- Deeper understanding of the bigger picture
- Enhanced sense of wellbeing
- Promotes psychic abilities
- Provides a sense of direction, fulfillment & inner harmony

"Try to be mindful, and let things take their natural course. Then your mind will become still like a clear forest pool."

Ajahn Chah

———

We are all part-physical and part-spiritual beings. Meditation helps us marry up those two elements of ourselves, making us 'whole'. We are then able to fire on all cylinders when dealing with whatever life throws at us.

Being a spiritual person isn't aligned or contrary to any particular religion. It is merely tapping into a 'given' part of ourselves. In today's world, being tuned into ourselves spiritually is becoming more important than ever before to keep us balanced and grounded.

Meditation, with its quietening and strengthening process, helps us face the truth, let go, move forward and continue to follow our path through life.

Dedicated to Sue Blake...

Our dearest friend, departed
Who shines among the stars
Your smile, unforgettable
Your presence felt

———

1.

journeying

*spiritual
awakening*

———

your strength, builds a life for you to flower

I am a maiden voyage

I am a maiden voyage
And I have a thirst for knowledge
I've travelled far and wide
In search of adventure and perhaps to hide
Away from my tormented past
It follows me wherever I go

At times I've felt depressed and low
But the storms pass and new horizons await
Full of promise, I willingly accept my new fate
For I'm a believer in nurture and nature

We are taught lessons that grow us as people
Sent into the wilderness so we can free flow
Find ourselves and renew our spirit
Life is a blessing, we are meant to live it

Remembering my troubled journeys and pain
Thunder and lightning brings the rain
The heavens open, it's a spectacular sight
The sun shines through, there's a bird in flight

I open my eyes, feel refreshed and alive
I know I've made it and survived

I'm a wild horse, I need to break free
Run through forests, fields, rushing water – be filled with glee
I've always had courage, I am a true fighter
I need to unburden my soul and feel lighter
Look ahead and see the summit

Cherish the stepping stones that brought me here
I no longer have anything to fear
I'll never forget the sharp daggers that drew blood
Will always carry the scars, but no longer flood

Of anguish and rejection, it was never my fault
No longer shall you hurt and rub in the salt
To create fresh wounds, make me bleed and deepen my injury
Instead I have to forgive, let go and feel sympathy

You know not what you do, you are lost
And I cannot reach through
I wish I knew how, but you failed
To protect me and instead you nailed

A steel door across your heart
Shutdown and withdrew
Into a dark place, that's cold and unsightly
I think of you daily and nightly

Love you in peace

You shattered my world, and blew me apart
But I've moved on and made a fresh start

Rebuilding my life, deep down you'd be proud
Sometimes I wish to scream aloud
What a waste of your life, it should have been different

I have to see through your layers of self-destruction
I seriously do not know how you still function
I know your love for me is real
Yet you're damaged beyond appeal
You run through me, I'll always treasure
The gifts you gave me in true measure

I miss the eyes that gazed on me lovingly
Adored me, we had a special bond
I used to think it impossible to be broken
But cruel experience has spoken

All I can do is lead a full enriched life
Let the breeze take me into a sweet lull
Kiss goodbye to my sorrows, I have much to give

Celebrate the stars, sea and moon
Rediscover the joys of the trees in the wood
Walk among valleys, cornfields and seeded rows
Or feel the golden light sands between my toes

Swim in the ocean and ride its waves
Let the tide take me to explore its hidden caves

I'm glad I am a soldier
Not of warfare, but of stature
Of standing tall, I will emerge
To provide light and a radiant surge
To others in need of help and guidance

To be a bright star that is my calling
To give to others instead of falling

Forgiveness is the key
A happy adventure is what I see
I am being beckoned to change winds
Brave the next chapter, it now sings

I hear a sweet melody, played on a harp
An angel appearing with wings and a smile
We are safe again, even though life can be a trial

But there's always a guide
In whom you can confide

Harmony and balance sweeps the dust away
Rest your head on my shoulder and lay
Sweet kisses, dewdrops, now play...

Turn with a different tide

Sail so that you feel
The gusts of winds against your raw skin
Your hair being blown ferociously
The rush of air against your body

Brushes you and clears the debris away
You are purified by nature's calling
Bellowing at you that you are alive
As your blood flows and circulates around you

The waves crash around the bow of the boat
Spittle splashes you so that you taste the salty sea water
Making you thirsty for more

And so the quell of the storm stills
And dusk falls, silence

All becomes calm and you clearly see

The voyage has rocked you
To turn with a different tide

Pearl in the sand

Look o'er my shoulder
We can't quite see
What will travel
In the yonder
But as we ponder

We can strengthen our core
While we look for the shore
Find our pearl in the sand
That glints in our hand

Spiritual awakening

When we have feelings of
dissatisfaction in our lives, there
is usually a very good reason. This
reason is a 'spiritual awakening.' It is
a transformation of our spiritual self
into another more progressive stage.

Awakening can be a painful and
uncomfortable struggle. It is
also ultimately liberating and
enlightening, even though it may
cause us to journey through a
quagmire of stomach-churning,
emotional instability, before we find
the courage to make the necessary
changes within ourselves to live our
lives honestly and happily.

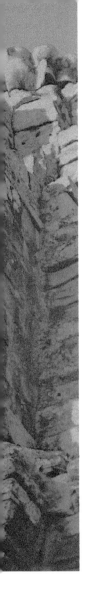

Signs and symptoms of a spiritual awakening:

- Letting go of tightly held beliefs and views
- Sensitivity to negative people, places and events
- Becoming aware of 'synchronicity' – the seemingly unrelated events and signs that we see and experience
- Wanting to break away from blind conformity, outdated institutions, unnecessary traditions and the status quo
- Greater self-awareness and awareness of the outside world
- A greater sense of inner peace, even though there may be moments of emotional turmoil

So what is the key to spiritual awakening?

Meditation is the only known way to increase the body's capacity to activate the scientifically proven quantum energy that is present during a spiritual awakening.

What do we gain with this spiritual awakening?

- A true sense of inner peace
- A sense of purpose
- Real happiness, no matter the situations occurring in our life
- A greater feeling of unconditional love towards all living beings
- Finding our true self and our true path
- A more fulfilled and meaningful life
- A permanent higher shift in consciousness and understanding

2.

forgiveness

*moving
forward*

————

my spirit emanates from my core

Empowerment

Why is this happening to me?
And why can't anyone see
The torrid currents
That run through my body
Causing me to cry out loud
But no one hears?

When the going gets rough
You question why life is tough
Your eyes get watery
Contortion your face to look sultry

A release of pain
You think you're insane
To have thoughts and fears
That tumble out in your tears
A display of despair
It seems so unfair

Fear is a treacherous place
Limbs jar, your mind frozen
Stops you moving forward

Keeps you in its tight claustrophobic reign
Puzzled and confused, you lose your way

Your confidence and self-belief ebbs
Downwards into a never ending abyss

Yet warning signs alert you to this danger
Your inner voice telling you not to cage her
Not to die a slow, unwitting death

A sudden jolt, a shudder, pulls you from the brink
A short sharp slap around the face
Awakens you, offering you a fresh perspective

It's ok, you can sink so low
Sometimes you have to go on a ride that's solo

Curling up, hibernating, it's the waiting that's agony
A piercing pain, a feeling that life has become a tragedy

Yet a symbol, a sign
A glimmer of life and a light that shines

I have only myself
To preserve my inner spirit
Hidden away, it slowly surfaces

And comes to my rescue
This is my sign, my cue

To rid those feelings of helplessness
I can cope nonetheless

My spirit emanates from my core
Until it floods me and tells me no more

Comforts me like a warm blanket
I look deep within and thank it

It's my own source of rich protection
I need to go on this journey of self-detection

To face the grief
And accept the thief

Who robbed me of so much
To be able to piece myself back together
I know this feeling of gloom can't last forever

I cast the darkness into a round ball
And kick it out into the bright moonlight and see it fall
Into a million white flashes

Of bursts of positive energy
Killing off my remnants of lethargy

I have become as light as a feather
I want to walk in fields of purple heather

My hardship will always be a stain
On my past, forever etched, it will remain

But this clouded silhouette
Invites me to step outside
Explore in search of exciting adventure

Gift of forgiveness

Make believe in yourself
You are sturdy and have stealth
Take on the knocks, twists and turns
Heal your sorrow, your pain, your churns

Of knots in your stomach, anxiety abounds
Quieted, stay still and silent, listen to the sounds
Peace and love within your heart you've found
Make undone the cruelty, forgiveness is the crown

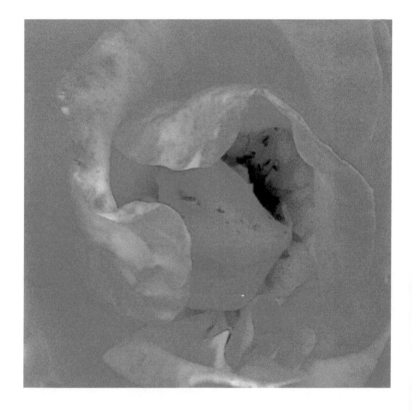

For forgiveness is the gift to tower
Your strength, builds a life for you to flower
To remain open and unburdened
Allow your petals to unfurl, not curtained

Breathe new wisdom and use it wisely
To care for yourself and not be feisty
To pour scorn and hatred you will only suffer
Away with your bitterness will make you tougher

To stand strong and proud in your surrounding
And offer comfort to those in need of soft landing
You will be leading a more enriched life
Instead of wanting to stick in the knife

How better to forgive and create positive impact
Than to lead a life of misery, in chains, kept intact
Revenge is an easy tool, don't be a fool
Far better to temper and remain cool

Reflect upon all the reasons
From multiple perspectives and seasons
Put yourself in the footsteps of those
To understand they're not your enemies or foes

They are lost, tortured and troubled
Face your own fears and then uphold
Values of virtue and forgiveness
For you are blessed to offer more, not less

Of abundant love, grow forth
And allow your soul to morph
Into a pixie, fairy, elf, travel north
Open the gates of your heart up into mind
It is simply our duty to be kind

Moving forward

———

Sometimes when the worst things happen to us, or what we perceive to be the worst things, we ask the question, *'Why? Why me? Why now?'*. Often the reasons seem unfathomable or entirely invisible.

For some strange reason, we human beings seem to enjoy holding onto feelings caused by negative events in our lives. There are of course occasions when this can be quite helpful in stopping us repeating mistakes, but it can also be harmful to hold onto the pain of a negative event.

We tend to cling to the emotions we felt, be it grief, horror, fear or perhaps a combination of them all. We seem to fear that by letting go of those emotions, we might forget and/or minimise the importance of that event.

However, if we hold onto these feelings and emotions for too long, they begin to colour everything in our lives and in time we even begin to define ourselves as, 'the person to whom this dreadful event happened'.

At this point we have stopped, and by that I mean we block ourselves from progressing with our lives.

Of course, nobody knowingly does this to themselves, but it can and does happen to people who are considered, and consider themselves to be balanced in every way.

It takes courage to acknowledge that this has occurred. It takes more courage and faith in the future to let it go. It is not impossible. It can be done.

The things that happen to us in life are usually there to help us learn the lessons we need to learn, helping us to evolve and progress. Sometimes these things have to be quite harsh in order for us to take the lessons on board sufficiently, to make the necessary changes within ourselves and to really move forward.

When something apparently catastrophic hits us, we initially reel with the shock. Then, a little further down the track, and if we are enlightened enough, we begin to see the reason(s), *'Why? Why me? Why now?'*

However 'bad' something or some happening may seem to be, it is always important to look at what we have learned from it and how others may have had to adjust their perspective as a result.

As just one example, perhaps we have broken unhelpful patterns of behaviour in ourselves and in others. These can be karmic patterns of behaviour, which may have been continuing from generation to generation.

We can then begin to see that the 'dreadful thing that has befallen us', has happened for an extremely positive reason. By strengthening ourselves to deal with it, we have also allowed others to strengthen and evolve in a way they might not have otherwise.

When life throws the unthinkable at us, it helps not at all to throw our hands up and say, 'I can't cope'. We have to cope or we sink.

There is always a lesson to be learned, no matter how hard or awful or horrendous or unbearable the experience we go through. And the lesson is always, without fail, worth learning.

All of us are stronger than we think.

Don't give up, ever.

3.

inner strength

self-esteem

———

a shooting star

Spider's web

A spider's web can be a tangle
Once caught, it's hard to unravel
Frost illuminates its intricate pattern
Contrasts starkly, threads like satin

A marvel of nature, glistening
But laid out to ensnare
Its unknowing victims'
Blood thirsting and hungry
Sucks the life out of your body

Those wise and clever
Watch from afar
Admiring its beauty

Until the web torn into a thousand shreds
A labour of love, vanished
But life goes on and the cycle
Continues, rebuilding and then fallen
Intended so that small pleasures
Can be found in the weariest of souls

When the web pins you down
Master the strength to tear it
Break its stronghold
Find its centre and remove the links
That weaken its presence
And becomes invisible
No longer to see

Inner violin

My soul is tortured
My insides scream
A feeling of emptiness
A holding of space

I am a vessel
I am a violin
Melodic to melancholic
Legato to staccato

There is a candle
That flickers
And lights my strings
The bow is steady again

And seamlessly forms
Into a continuous charming note
A lullaby, an inner voice
Echoes around the heart chambers

Resets your body clock
And chimes with a twinkle

A shooting star
Re-energises the soul
And pulls you up again
Feel its release from your crown

Cycle of self-realisation

You're a no hoper
At least that's what you think
The crowds you surround yourself with
Make you feel your mind's a sieve

Why do you listen to their tales of negative woe
Accept the curses they lay at your door
Why do you take on their insults
Wear them like a cloak and remain in their shadow?

Weighing you down like lead
Full of metal, solid, so your soul feels dead
Unfeeling and unkind
Cold and icy
That sends shivers down your spine

Your heart has become hardened
You have nothing left to give
Of not your friends, people judge you
So you scorn them more instead

But deep down it confirms
You're a no hoper
At least that's what you think
Stuck in the mire

You're giving nothing away
Pretend you don't care
That others look and squirm at you
Hating you instead

Is this really what you want
Life is hard to bear
To keep up the appearance
You really do not care

Perhaps it's time to confess
To someone who can help
Who will listen and address your issues
Let your tears roll down into tissues

Remove the lead that weighs you down
Remove the wrinkles and the frown
No longer do you shiver
Nor have a heavy heart

The friends you lost were curses
Draining from your self-esteem purses
No longer are you a no hoper
A coper you are instead

No longer stuck in the mire
Or pretending you don't care
Of your feelings, you've learnt to share

People no longer squirm at you
Instead they warm to you
Your heart you've defrosted
No longer full of metal

No longer are you a no hoper
A motivator you are instead
You see the same pattern in others
Holding a mirror to their face
And when they say they're useless
You tell them they have a choice

It's all about perception you see
I see in you, you as me
They tell you they're a no hoper
At least that's what they think

Until you tell them otherwise
As you wait to hear their cries

Self-esteem

Taking stock is good for us.

We simply must make time to
review the key areas of our lives
on a regular basis.

Busy people have no trouble in doing
even more work but find it very hard
making time for themselves: for some
it's as if work and other peoples'
needs are way more important than
their own.

How can this be right?

——

As a consequence of 'busy busy busy', bad habits are created which may not be acknowledged until they trip us up and force us to STOP.

It is often only then that we acknowledge and admit to ourselves that we have some big issues to deal with. The trick is prevention and this is honed through self-awareness and self-respect.

To be healthily selfish is a good thing. Today's world places high demands on our physical body, our mind, our emotions and our self-esteem. The purpose of taking stock at regular intervals is to check in with how you are doing to spot the craters and do something about them, before you fall in.

What we do for a living is important but it shouldn't define who we are. We are all more than the work we choose. Behaving like a hamster on a wheel and a perpetual rabbit in headlights isn't a good way to live. I can promise you, if you don't take control of your life's rhythm and output, it will take control of you.

Key areas to take stock of on a regular basis are:

- The quality of your home and working environments
- Key relationships: family, friends and colleagues – do they sustain or drain?
- Determine the quality of your emotional, physical and mental health
- What unhelpful habits/behaviour have you collected?
- What are you *tolerating* in all areas of your life?
- What's your personal care regime like – do you even have one?
- How healthy is your self-esteem and self-respect?

Live like your life depends on it. Tolerating what's rubbish in our lives is living a lie.

4.

guided wisdom

clarity of thought

———

bestows power of harmony and peace

The silver moonlit stag

In the silver light, a stag darts out from under the forest canopy
Antlers held high, mystical in its silent stance
Stares in authority, alert and knowing
Eyes interlocked, sees me and sends signals

A calmness descends across the night dusky mist
Where the dew has settled on the leafy forest floor
Of springy soft, shimmery silk grass
Fragrant and damp under my bare feet
And time is suspended, as we fixate

While I collect my thoughts and ruminate
Spellbound by this sacred, ancient creature
That bestows its power of harmony and peace

I breathe in the fresh air
Observe him as he observes me, gracefully
He is my majestic charm, into my soul he looks
He understands me – feels what I feel

His presence is reassuring
His air of solace carried by the winds
Touches upon my heart
Soothes it, and suddenly I see for myself
My own strength, my own courage, my own gifts

He has come as my guide, my messenger
To bring me wisdom and enlightenment
A sigh of relief releases from my lips
Expelling the thoughts that have sorrowed my soul

A singular tear of joy appears in the corner of my eye
A teardrop crystalised by the light of the bright stars
Made up of a million constellations
And a million performances, dance
To celebrate all that I am

And in loving myself
I can be kind and gentle
I can travel to my quiet space of tranquillity
For here, I remember who I am
In this space, I can hear clearly, my received wisdom

Wand of life

A treasure trove of emeralds, rubies and sapphires
Sets the heart off and lights its fires
An inner cove of goblets, trinkets and stones
A labyrinth of fineries to decorate the most elaborate of thrones

Fit for a king or queen, there's more
To discover layers upon layers, until you're sure
You've dug deep and hit the bottom of the crest
A wand to behold, cradled in its nest

Holds powers, righteous, glints and catches the eye
Steadies the breath until you escape with a sigh
Brings it to life with its mirth, gold, heavy to touch
Wizened, knows deep secrets of folklore and such

Plays music, mellow sounds that are authoritative
A prize for the keeping, it will be supportive
If you don't abuse, but love it infinitely
Will allow you to create notes, build your own symphony

Let it plot out your journey
Till the end of your life with it, bow out with a courtesy
You've lain it close to your chest
Rewarded you with love, provided you with peace and rest

A comfort and joy, you've danced its merry tune
Now it's time to impart, pass it on, no it's not come too soon
Spread the harmony and its offering
Begin a new following
Its spirit lives on, through you

Clarity of thought

——

To be able to manage our lives, our circumstances and ourselves (the good, the bad and the ugly), there has to be a place of retreat, a sanctuary where we rest our minds and quieten sufficiently to bring in much needed clarity. If our minds are noisily racing and cluttered, how on earth can we have clarity?

I often wonder why we are so drawn to the circular and frequently negative arguments that consume our brains. These force out the intuitive guidance that every one of us can tap into if we quieten enough to reach it and recognise it.

Meditation becomes a sanctuary, a retreat, a 30-minute pool of bliss within our hectic day.

We are creating a positive step enabling us to replenish ourselves and make space for measure, balance and clarity of thought. All these things allow us to manage the impossibly fast pace of our day, together with managing our moods, our circumstances and our lives.

5.

charms of protection

understanding our light

—————

you are light

Light

Shadows appear and fade, light prevails
Darkness descends, only to be swept away by light

For light is radiant, bright, provides hope

Darkness is heavy, wears you down, burdens the soul
Light is abundant, if you realise your dreams, follow your heart, your intuition

Even at dusk, there is a pool of milky white
The face of the moon, smiling down on us even in the darkest hour
No need to be scared, frightened, or fearful
Let the light guide you to safety. Peace be upon you

For the light provides you a blanket of comfort
Feel wrapped up in warmth, love and tranquillity
You are light. You are pure. You are radiant

You, are safe

White feathers

A sea of white feathers
And tiny soft balls of light
Glide and travel past you

Of guardian angels
They brush against your skin
Your charms of protection

Whispering in lullabies
And the sounds of playful giggles
Soothing your worried thoughts

What seems heavy darkness sitting on your heart
Is just an illusion of your mind
If you look out

For signs of wholesomeness and goodness
Righteousness surpasses wrongdoing
Love, honour, integrity and purity

Creates a beacon of courage, bravery and leadership
To stand up for yourself and the rights of others
Being a guide, bringing hope and peace

To those who have been wronged
And pillaged by ruthlessness
Yet, still the white feathers appear

Before your very eyes to provide
Protection against these evil actions
But do not hate or feel victimised

As this journey reveals its lessons to you
To deepen your strength and resolve of character
To learn to overcome and fight

These battles from a place of true intention
To overcome fear of intimidation
So that your morals and soul remain intact

No-one, but no-one can remove the moral fibres
That lay like an intricate, delicate, woven fabric
Of resilience within you, untouchable

Surround yourself with loving healing and light
Feel the curses of others
Who have dared to parasite your mind

Be removed and released from your crown
And sit in quiet contemplation
Breathe sighs of relief and relax

You feel nothing but virtue
And are restored
To your own being of true light

Understanding our 'light' & avoiding it being stolen

___

We, as human beings, emanate an energy or vibration. This is called our 'light' because it comes from a place within us of pure goodness and love. It is both a physical and spiritual energy, which we all have, to some extent or another. Our light comes from our essence and is our good intention towards others.

Some people have this 'light', this good energy, in abundance. Although it is not visible to the majority of people (and there are many people who can see auras), it is nonetheless very noticeable and something people 'sense' the very moment they come into contact with it.

How often do you find yourself in the company of people who drain your energy?

All of us have people in our lives who seem to suck all the energy out of us. These people are usually very needy. They are attracted to our 'light' like moths to a flame and, although we may try to support them, nothing is ever quite enough for them. They always seem to need that little bit more, and then even a bit more still. In the end it is we who are left depleted, drained of our energy, our 'light'.

Energy-draining people do not necessarily figure in our personal or professional lives in a regular way. We may meet them fleetingly, but just a short time in their company can leave us feeling zapped, wondering what hit us.

The light never goes away from us – we go away from it!

How often do we find ourselves trying to maintain and sustain toxic relationships? This can be within a marriage or partnership, within the workplace or within our family and friendships. The relationship itself is so very evidently out of balance but we are still hanging on in there, propping up the other person. In effect, our 'light' is being stolen.

We should be very aware that
we too, can often be drawn and
attracted to people with negative
energy. Sometimes these people
can sense our 'light' and would like
to own it themselves, although this
is not usually a conscious thought
or intention on their part.

Negative energy is frequently cloaked
by such charisma and charm that
initially we are intoxicated and our
normal 'sight' and rationale in that
moment is lost. No matter how
charismatic or charming someone
might be, the art of seeing beyond
this is important.

- Why do some of us repeat the
  pattern again and again, often
  being attracted to these negative
  types of people?

- Why do many of us find we
  continually fall for the same kind
  of person when that relationship
  has been unsuccessful?

It is because we are attracted to an
energy/vibration which is familiar to
us. This can just as easily be a negative
energy or vibration as a positive one. The
point here is that the energy is familiar to
us and we then, mistakenly, think we are
attracted to it. Because the attraction
and familiarity can be so strong at times,
our rational brain is deluded.

- So how can we recognise this and break the repeating pattern?

- How can we better manage situations to regulate the amount of time and the direction in which we expend that energy?

We need to manage ourselves around needy/energy-sapping people. It begins with developing self-awareness that helps us to recognise, accept and confront the truth of our relationships and situations.

When quietened at a deep soul level, we enter what I call the 'truth zone'. This is a place where we cannot escape the truth. It isn't optional: it's what happens when we connect to our higher self; we connect to ourselves at soul level, reaching a knowledge which is far wiser and more profound than anything the mind can produce.

We develop and heighten our innate
sixth sense, our intuition, which then
enables us to 'see' beyond the shell
of a person, beyond what they are
presenting to us and that they would
have us believe. We see them for
who and what they truly are and we
develop the courage and the will to
protect ourselves.

We grow our self-esteem, self-respect
and self-love. We literally cultivate our
internal source of positive energy.

We begin to manage our life by
actually letting go of the reins of
control, gaining the courage to face
the facts rather than trying to force
things to live up to the illusion we
have created with our minds.

We enhance our ability to 'see' people
for who they truly are and, in time,
we notice a shift in our thinking and
behavioural responses. We achieve
a truer perspective and develop the
confidence to either distance ourselves
or entirely let go and move away
from who or what is stealing our 'light'!

6.

realise your dreams

letting go

———

walk through the doorway...

Your field of dreams awaits you...

I hear these negative voices
Fear prevents me from making my own choices
I have my dreams
Trickling streams

I make excuses
I choose to be elusive
That way I don't have to face
The questions of others who chase

My own dreams away
Who will take seriously what I have to say
So I submerge them instead
Yet a burning desire is fed

Rips through my body
But still, I continue to deny me
It's easier to take the safer route
Block out my own sounds and remain on mute

Bury my head in the sands
While I contemplate, dream of other lands
Create fantasies as escapism
Look through the keyhole of my own prism

Adventures galore
Opportunities lure
On the other side
For too many years I have shied

Locked myself in and built a shell
But as I peek out, a thought soon fell
What if I lift the lid and walk through the doorway
Realise my own possibilities and that I may

Step outside and breathe in the fresh air
Filling my own lungs with happiness and share
My own thoughts and feelings and question those who dare
Challenge my dreams, I am now beyond care

What others think and the pressures placed
To fit in with their expectations, to suit their taste
It's no longer fair to judge me, I shout and declare
I am my own person, I no longer remain in your lair

I am free at last, at one with the elements
I have to walk forth and use my own intelligence
Of carving out my own footpath
I wrestle with negative chatter and laugh

I have outgrown you, I'm done with the past
I am majestic, now I have to move fast
No time to lose, there's no time like the present
To love myself and create my own crescent

I reclaim the parts of me
The windows of my soul see
A life I can now live
Where I have so much more to give

Pooling my gifts
Will offer my inner being a world of lifts
What's happening to me inside
This torrent of self-love presides

Flowing through me like a river
Make my wishes come true so I can deliver
My energy, spirit and charisma

If I continue to ignore, I'll always be forlorn
I am now witness to my own new dawn
The magnitude of bringing my dreams together
Means a life fulfilled forever

Authentic pathway

Traipsing through dirt tracks, fjords and untrodden paths
It's time for you to take off the mask
To realise the authentic pathway
It seems so faraway
But yet it's near
The cost of avoiding it is dear

To waste life's opportunity
Of feeling such affinity
Speak your truth, you can no longer hide
Behind closed doors and pretend it's not there
Obstacles and challenges to be overcome
But no longer see it as cumbersome

On learning the immediate position, don't retreat
Even though you think it's easier to give in to defeat
To walk away, too complicated, what are you to do
This trigger that travels your soul through and through

Should you pretend it didn't exist
This veil of mystery descended in mist

Now you've reached deeper levels
Dig deep to dishevel
The safety net you have created
Part of your past that deviated

You away from your true sense of self
The heavy weight of responsibility
You at first sight saw the futility

Of a hard life, worn down and beaten
Made you feel lonely, it was unfair
That life drove you to deep despair

Coping mechanisms set in motion
You're now at a crossroads unravelling this notion

Of the strategies you put in place
To make you feel safe

Yet at odds with your nature
You have to find peace with your maker
Unweave the knots and loosen
Release the energy to flow
You are ready again to grow

A wishing well

The penny drops
As you visualise a dream
Your heart palpitates
Hands clamped, your mind calculates

Will it come true because you desire
This wish that feeds a fire
So huge it's planetary
But excitement is momentary

Quickly fizzles out, it's impossible, just a dream
Yet you wait to hear as the coin falls
Through the deep rounded dark walls

Your wish has landed, waiting
An eternity for you, baiting
You to act upon it, in this lifetime

That coin remains still until the water stirs
As other peoples' dreams and wishes whir
Among yours, waiting patiently

And as you forget the wish you made in that well
It remembers you because it's your permanent token
Borne by your motion

A thrust of energy
Makes a melody
It's your tune
To dance and play out

The coin, glinting below the surface
Forever remains your wish
Daring for you to fish
For your wish to come true…

Letting go

——

Letting go requires a leap of faith. Letting go means having faith in the future. Faith that you will heal, cope and move on as you need to. It is a fact that by choosing to release ourselves from what we have outgrown and weighs us down, or is just not good enough for us, is a pre-requisite for emotional balance and the opportunity to live a full and happier life. If it was easy everyone would do it, yet the practice of letting go is not actually as difficult as you think, particularly when our mindset is conducive to allowing change.

Fear and lack of self-esteem plays a major part in why we stay within difficult personal and professional relationships, spend time with toxic 'friends', hold onto self-sabotaging habits and behaviour, and stay in unfulfilling jobs and unsupportive environments. Fear of the unknown and stepping out of our comfort zone holds us back. What a bizarre term of reference 'comfort zone' is, when, for many people, what they are so tightly clinging to is far from comfortable.

Holding on for dear life to what causes us pain, discomfort and no longer supports us is not going to enhance our journey through life.

In fact, choosing not to 'let go' can lower or destroy our self-esteem and drain our energy. Not letting go affects our health, enthusiasm, vitality and zest for life and may well affect the next decision we make for ourselves, and possibly our families.

Equally important, until we let go we inhibit the next stage of our journey through this life and if, for example, it is a person to whom we are clinging albeit within an unhappy relationship, we inhibit their path too.

Here are some examples of things we tend not to let go of:

- Marriages and partnerships which have completely broken down
- Toxic and needy 'friends' who drain our energy
- Environments in which we are no longer comfortable, fulfilled or appreciated. This might be at work or where we spend time relaxing, even the home we live in
- Illusions: this can be the illusion of being in love with someone, or that a particular person is our friend when they prove themselves not to be
- Unhappiness and the past: time to let it go and move on
- Bereavement: we tend to cling to feelings of grief, not realising that we are fearful of letting it go. Grief was the last emotion we felt at the time this loved one died and we subconsciously fear that by letting it go, we will lose our last link to that person. The truth, however, is that we never lose that link. By letting go, we are then able to look back with love and laughter at the times we have shared with the person we have lost.

Let's say we need to have a conversation with someone who has been offensive in their behaviour towards us. If our mind is quietened, we are able to get past our own heightened emotions (initial flight or fight response) and we find the words to convey our message in a measured yet firm way, with due compassion and respect for the other party, while not losing our self-respect by spitting venom through intense feelings of anger, frustration or hurt.

Speaking about an emotional subject in this measured way will ensure we are listened to, heard and better understood. A more harmonious result is likely to follow.

Letting go is not only about the ending of relationships. We hold onto so many things that are not doing us much good.

Our work is just one other example. There are obvious and practical reasons why we stay in our place of work, especially if we have dependents. However, there is always a way to change any situation if we explore our possibilities and then have the courage to act upon our findings, to set things in place.

Perhaps we have decided that a change of workplace or career is the only possibility but are too fearful to make the move. The next stage would be to take time to gather information, create a plan of action and lay foundations, before actually quitting our present employment.

With a quietened mind we will be more able to navigate through this change, making the transition smoother, less traumatic and overall far more comfortable – all achieved by *letting go* of the fear.

"Learn to let go
This is the key to happiness."

Buddha

―――――

self-awareness

strengthening

———

earthly and damp, you feel rooted

Silver birch

Dig deep in the soil
With the earth that doth coil
Plant yourself with your feet first, it's a miracle
Look up to the sky, leaves rushing by, it's spherical

Earthly and damp, you feel rooted
Wholesome and loving, it's not convoluted
We are the gift, life brought us here
Why do we waste so much energy trying to disappear?

It's a simple thought
So often we are caught short
Where we grapple for air
But in the circle we share

So we can feel light and airy
A laugh, a shudder, a cry, it's not that contrary
To pull our strengths together, it's not tragic
To believe we can create magic

I have a silver birch in my hand
So as one whole unity we can put in land
Our dreams, and hopes, may we bless this sapling
With its roots we feel grounded and go trampling

As we leave here and walk the four corners of the earth
Forever we remain connected
So that we are constantly protected

By this tree of life
Our hearts and souls beat as one
Our memory of our time here, will always live on

Safe passage

In a far, far, faraway land
For thousands of miles of sand
A traveller stood
Knowing he could
Choose his destiny over fate

By looking up to the skies
He would then shut his eyes
And work out all the possibilities
Daring not to tread where
Hidden dangers in the desert may fare

For his life depended on it to reach safety
He would remain calm, from dusk till dawn
Letting his feet sink into the golden lawn
Of warmed up tiny nuggets
And put his thoughts into different buckets

When morning arose
One of his buckets had froze
Telling him his next course of action
Which were always sound of mind
The right solution, he would always find

So the lesson here
To hold very dear
Is to remain still
Instead of turning ill

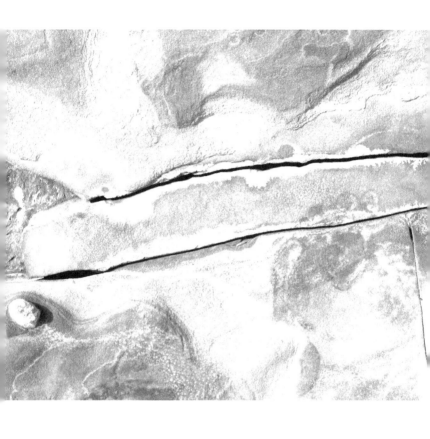

With worry it's too fraught
Don't get caught
Off guard by making an irrational decision
Give yourself solitude
It saves to be patient and work out your longitude

Your next crossing
Wishes you safe longing
And a heart of compassion
To keep on moving in a fashion

And strike out your continued footsteps with meaning
So you can reach your new goal with awakened feeling
Of excitement and joy, instead of sorrow and woe

Now feel free
Light, and you will see
The bright blazing horizon
Beckoning you to walk forward
To take on this adventurous passage

Follow the breath of your kite

Up in the valleys
Dizzying heights
And the kites
Catch the winds
Carried away
Into the thermos of the air

Their wings in free movement
Taking off, then dipping
Its soul dancing with the music
Beauty with the elements
A delicate hand, extends its reach
To take hold of its line

So it can balance you
Witness its new shapes
Against the skyline and clouds
And its pull, inviting you
To play, a moment
For pause and reflection

You are that kite, interlocked
It takes you on a journey
For if you follow its breath
It will guide you with its energy
Because it knows
Where to head

With cries of joy and laughter, rejoice
In that simple pleasure of flying your kite
Don't lose its magical touch

Feeling free and light
And never lose sight
Of that natural child
That enjoys the surroundings of fresh air

Take yourself away from pollution
In that kite, you'll find your solution

Strengthening

———

A weak external economy requires us to
take a more grounded, solid and stable
approach to our lives. It is not what
happens to us, it is how we react and deal
with it that counts.

- Do you often find that you have
  unwittingly backed yourself into a
  corner or feel you have grasped the
  short straw in life?
- Do you sometimes feel emotionally
  weak and not in control?
- Do situations run away with you
  when all you were trying to do was
  lend a helping hand?
- Do you perpetually struggle with
  yourself regarding what your own
  motives are within a given situation?

When we feel we are going through
life getting curve balls thrown at us
repeatedly, we sometimes gravitate
towards a lowered emotional place
as it, perversely, feels a 'safe' place
to stay. When we are in that lowered
emotional state, we fail to recognise
that we are repeating patterns of
unhelpful responses to the situations
that confront us. Conversely, our
reactions and behaviour can sabotage
the very outcome we are seeking.

We all have choices in life and it is our
choice whether or not we do the work
to strengthen ourselves. Every one
of the actions we take each day has a
consequence in some way. There is a cause
and effect – or karma – in everything we
do and the energy we create by taking an
action will come back to us in some way
and at some point.

When we are highly emotionally charged,
the decisions we make for ourselves
and others are frequently clouded and
therefore are often impaired.

The phrase 'the buck stops here' springs
to mind. When we gain the courage to
confront ourselves squarely and honestly,
there is nowhere to hide. We must, at this
point, meet our emotional selves head on.
Can there be a more perfect opportunity in
this life to ensure we get it right?

Increased resolve helps us *see* the 'signs'
and *read* them correctly. We become
stable and perceptive at our very core. We
truly learn to take control of our own lives.

A sharpness of mind allows us to:

- **Objectively** analyse situations, assess people and motives with the correct perspective and without the emotions that cloud our thoughts and colour our views in an unhelpful way
- **Achieve** the ability to bring balance into our lives and become more effective in a high-performance working world
- **Develop** the courage to say 'no' and 'yes' for the right reasons
- **Grow** in confidence, which gives us the ability to remain unfazed over things that would once have knocked us off balance
- **Build** the courage to establish healthy boundaries, which also earns us the respect of others
- **Create** strength to 'let go' of unhelpful people or situations having developed a certainty about our decisions
- **Learn** to trust and draw upon our new-found inner strength and become free of self-limitations, because we have finally faced and accepted the truth about ourselves and our situations

Strengthening not only makes us more self-assured, happier and more fulfilled, but the ripple effect of our grounded persona, positively affects all those with whom we interact. People report that their personal and professional lives significantly improve.

follow your rainbow

overcoming fear

bloom in a garden of your own making

A heart of roses

When mountaintops tower high
They are not there to close you in
Nor cloak your body in an envelope of clouded mist

Yet standing too long, in a dampened spot
Will eventually let the winds and rain
Seep into your skin and turn it icy cold

Until you shiver with fear and lose your fight
So best to fear not, place foot forward
The winds and rain are your friend

Pushing and pulling you to cleanse you
Of your troubles and purifying your spirit
Loosening and washing away the debris

That has been unsettling you
Become gallant and proud
Of your achievements there are many

While those enemies of men and women
Who have taken up arms of greed
Pointing a chaliced arrow ready to poison your heart

They are makers of cowardly combat
Stand firm and strong
Let the winds be your guiding force

And the rain trickles over
Like a shower of liberation
Until the last droplets evaporate

Into distant vapours
And the pale-lit sky
Turns into a fire of auburns and reds

Purples and lavender, roses and dusky pinks
A rainbow of colours flash
And while you still feel scared

Your rainbow has appeared before you
To lead you over the hilltops and through the valleys
The ups and downs

Protecting you by creating a boundary
Between the world where others
Bestow on you their ill judgement

And a new land of opportunity
While it cannot be seen, smelt
Or it's direction known as yet

It will be your valley of life
Rather than to lie in the valley of death
It's not an option

To be a prisoner
Captured by those who feel
The power to control you

Is greater than your own
Do not allow yourself to become
Weakened by their threat of terror

For it has no home in you
Rendering your enemies' power useless
Use its force to champion you on

In your own quest to find purpose
By changing the nature of this power at source
Will be your blessing

To a brighter future
Just keep on seeing and believing
In the kaleidoscope of your rainbow

To bring you forth to your kingdom
Where you will crown your own glory
Instead of letting others steal

What is rightfully yours
For you are your own castle to govern
Lock your gate and draw up

Against your enemies
And welcome in kindness
With a fanfare of trumpeters

To mark your happy occasions
And celebrations of success
With a feast of friendship

Feel your spirit grow into a ball of light
Banish the darkness of others
Leave them to battle their own conscience

As your own courtyard is waiting
For you to plant your own seeds
To flower and bloom

In a garden of your own choice and making
That sunflower you imagined
Is now a reality

Reach out and up to touch it
It's golden leaves rich from the vibrant sun
Offer you sanctuary, peace and tranquillity

For the seed you planted many moons ago
Matured over countless time, patient
Knowing you will eventually be free
To garden your own kingdom of roses

Buttercups

When thou call to me
Thy speaks to me in spirit
A higher kingdom doth exist
Beyond the scope of thy consciousness
For there is a heavenly symbol
That floats above the parapet

A sign that rankles us forth
From our state of paralysis
Frozen, scared to draw breath, take a footstep forward
Stuck in oblivion, hiding, taking shelter in darkness
Yet, a torch, that emits sparkles
Dislodges us from our shrunken stupor

Cloaked in the shadows
An unknowing force that drives and propels us forwards
Trust in it, holds your hand firmly
Leading you to safety
Relinquish your tears
Straighten your shoulders
Grow tall, take in a deep breath

A white dove invisible to your eye
Flutters at your shoulder, guiding you
Along the winding path, past its jagged edges
And the high mountain of heavy drab grey slabs
That locked in the rivers of your heartfelt sorrow
Let it now flow through the underground

Past the grey enclosure, where you have lain trapped
Imprisoned in your own cave
And as you allow these floodgates to open
See the water gush forcefully seeking pastures new
Trickling into the cracks of the concrete
Until the surge builds, pummels and bursts through
Crumbling it to dust

That gives way to a lush rolling meadow
Poppied with warm buttercups that melt the icy waters
Into a barmy thermal spring
To bathe and soothe the pain away
Feel your body get lighter

As the golden, burnt orange sun blushes against your skin
Its heat permeating through your fingers and toes and travels through
Until your cheeks expand into a never ending smile

And now having stepped out from the gloom
You are once again free to celebrate your soul
Like the shedding of a skin
Your layers of grief-stricken servitude discarded

314 · follow your rainbow

As a new skin forms
Renewed, revitalised and re-energised
Your legs now as sturdy as wizened tree trunks
Rooted and earthed, but your arms hath flight
Ready to embrace life

For if you stop to listen
The singing of bluebirds calling you
To make the next footprint in a track of your own making

314 · follow your rainbow

As a new skin forms
Renewed, revitalised and re-energised
Your legs now as sturdy as wizened tree trunks
Rooted and earthed, but your arms hath flight
Ready to embrace life

For if you stop to listen
The singing of bluebirds calling you
To make the next footprint in a track of your own making

Gold-dust

A sea of stardust
Mystical, absorbing droplets of sparkles
Sprinkling down through the heavens
Bronzing your skin
Making you glow

Overcoming fear

———

Fear is created by the mind.
Fear creates an obstacle and we are
either knocked off track or we are
stuck and going nowhere.

Fearful thinking can literally immobilise us, making us feel paralysed, lost and frightened. We, as human beings, tend to over-analyse almost any situation or any happening in our lives, looking for and finding reasons to be fearful.

Fear sometimes comes in as an 'indicator' to protect us.

Isn't it odd then that it is fear we are trying to banish? Of course, if something terrible happens such as witnessing a car crash then you would be entitled to feel frightened. Yet feeling full of fear is not a healthy state – it is not good for your physical health or your relationships.

Living by our own truth

_____

We lose self-consciousness as we become less fearful and more secure within ourselves. It is not that we 'don't care' what other people think of us, but we become more confident in who we are and feel much more self-assured. Therefore living by our own truth and standards matters more to us than what others think of us.

Many people report that:

- They handle life better whatever happens
- Stressful situations seem to bother them less
- Challenging people and frustrations wash over them more easily than they did before

Think of the freedom this affords us. How liberating.

From a parenting perspective, it is important that we teach our children to understand about fear and intuition, so that they can grow up better equipped to handle their physical and emotional reactions to fear-inducing situations.

We are role models for our children. They mimic their parents, so the more grounded, quietened and measured in our behaviour we are, the better for them and in fact for everyone.

"I learned that courage was not the absence of fear, but the triumph over it. The brave man is not he who does not feel afraid, but he who conquers that fear."

Nelson Mandela (1918-2013)

9.

insight
& vision

enlightenment

———

follow your vision and intuition

Shoal of gifts

Lantern, lights the way
Gliding, floating, hovering
The breeze whispers to it
Slowly gathering momentum
It sees not its end destination
But travels along a seamless flow
Serene, taking in the scenery below

Observing life while all the same
Reaping what it sows
Flashing its sparkles as it glows
Helping others lives to grow
To be fulfilled in their creation
Of offering peace it came

To be realised that we are all the sum
Of one whole planet, universe, earth
We all tread upon its very turf
That feeds us life, its sovereign
We all reach out and help one another
To provide every individual with cover
Enough to plant seeds and mother

It is only fair we don't just sit
To leave it to others to have their say
We must all take action and joint responsibility
For facilitating change of lost mobility

The time is now, its ripe, it's here
We can't afford to rest on our laurels and just fear
Reach in and realise, dig deep from your soul
That your dreams, wishes, gifts, are your shoal
Have heart, courage and conviction
To follow your vision and intuition

Majestic wings

When thou hast wings
That have been clipped
Ask yourself

Who allowed you
To get caught
Was it you

Or did you
Allow others
To stop your feathers
From fluttering

Did you seek shelter
Away from braving the world
In full flight for all to see

Yet, you feel safer
Surrounded by the walls
That hide you

You are fed and watered
While others rule you
A false pretence of security

Then, lightening strikes
Tearing down the bricks
As they smash around you

And all you had
Built up around you
Destroyed

Exposed
The elements
Beating at you
To take flight

Your feathers ruffled
You are forced
To free yourself

Your majestic wings
Slowly fan out like a crest
A shield, against the battering

Until you let go
And honour yourself
Love yourself

Absorb molecules of pure air
Allowing your lungs
To breathe in the oxygen
That feeds
Your body with life and vigour

Swoop low
Soar high
Spin somersaults

Feel the wind-stream
Glide you to safety
While you enjoy
The joyful frivolity of the current

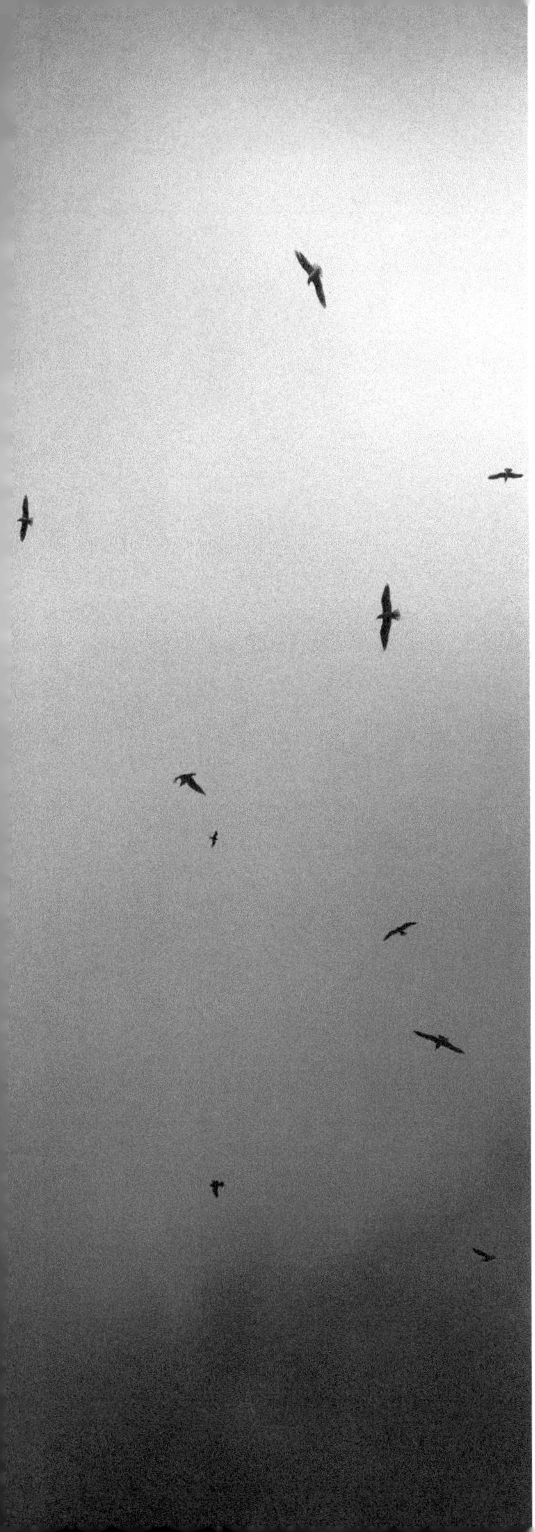

That allows you to travel
In a direction that brings
You home to your own nest

Full of comfort
Reconstructed
With your own loving care

In surroundings
Where all the elements
Are in alignment
To nourish your soul

Knowing your landing
Is soft, light, cosy
With no-one in sight
To harm you

From a circular cove
In a cliff-face
You see

The sea stretch out
With flowing waves
In rhythm
With your own heartbeat

Served by the tide
The moon, the sun
And the heavens

Your crest is your fortune
Your shield, your protection
Your feathers, of finest spun silk

The threads of life
So delicate
Yet woven strong

You can create
Any masterpiece
Of your choosing

You can rise, rise, rise
Channel your energies
To now be uplifted

Fly, fly, fly
Fly now

You see wonderment
In the world
You feel ready to explore

You have fire in your carriage
That carries you
To undiscovered frontiers

Waiting for you
In full glory
Laden with gifts

To reward you
For being kind to yourself
For acting

On the positive messages
You have been listening to
And receiving

Your inner beauty
Acknowledged by you
And now, by others

A land of magic
Within you
Awaits...

Liberation

My breath is pure
My soul replenished
Full of light and wisdom
I am returned anew

Strengthened in my core
My shoulders light
Airy, free and liberated
I am strong and stand tall

I am enlightened
With clarity and focus
My mind no longer awash
With heavy dark clouds

No longer is my mind clogged
With a foggy mess
A sea of unhealthy emotions
I have cleansed
Rinsed away the darkness

I am free

Free to see clearly
A bright happy future
Full of joy, love and laughter
It's time now to rejoice

Era of enlightenment

———

From a young age, we are taught how to deal with everyday life. We have to achieve, learn to overcome difficulties and pain, 'to stand up for ourselves' and move forward through our daily lives. It usually means we are so busy with learning to live in the physical, that our spiritual self takes a back seat and is frequently left there.

It doesn't matter at all what your religious beliefs are. I feel that what I teach transcends religions. I work with the light, spirit and love. It is the core of my work.

Everything I do comes from a place
of love and compassion. That is what
I try to impart to others through this
work. It is needed today as much as
in any turbulent time in history.

The world is full of diversity, so how can there only be one way? It's not possible. Tolerance is so important. We need to allow for differences, this is what makes the world such a fascinating place.

There have been wars in the world from time immemorial. Now again, we also have terrorism, frequently carried out in the name of religion. It's time for this to stop. The only way I can see war and terrorism being wiped out for good is through this message being spread continuously and worldwide.

We have evolved and will continue to
evolve as human beings. We're going
through a transitional period, which
always brings turmoil.

There has been so much recent disaster. It is the human race that makes war, not Spirit. We have *free choice* to listen to our innermost intuitive voice or be swayed by negative outside influences and peer pressure.

However, this is an era in which increasing numbers of people are coming to the conclusion that the message of compassion, understanding, thoughtfulness and, most of all, acceptance will unite people globally.

This is a beginning of a new era of people wanting to do good and wanting to unite, to bring care and shelter to others unable to care for themselves.

Spirit is there to help us, but spirit isn't answerable for everything. As human beings, we have *free will* and make our own choices. My choice has always been to follow the guidance that I am given. I know I'm not here to make miracles happen or put the world to rights by myself. I certainly can't walk on water but I can still spread the enlightenment I have gained.

If we all adopt a global mind, we can grow into something much bigger and better. There's no end to what we can achieve, maybe not in my lifetime, maybe not in our children's lifetimes, but certainly in generations to come.

It starts with accepting our neighbours, no matter their religion, creed or colour. Then the ripples will naturally follow and a movement of peace begins.

There will always be greed and there
will also be egos. We're never going to
wipe out negativity completely, but we
can make inroads into spreading as
much positivity as we can.

Where there's dark, there's light. Where
there's good, there's bad. Where there's
positive, there's negative – but we
can be fundamental in spreading
the message of enlightenment.

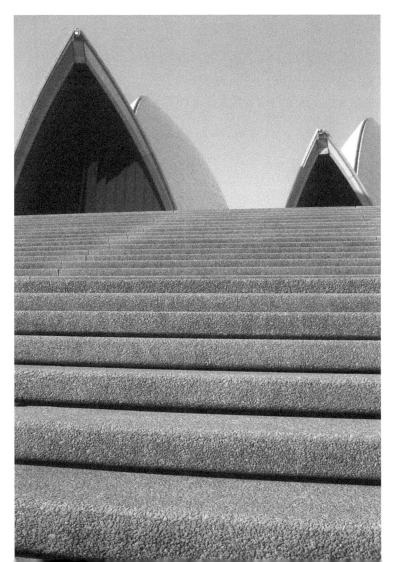

pained relationships

acceptance

———

time for planting new seeds

Pools of love

I am filled with sadness
Instead of joy and gladness
My heart aches
Love outpours into pools of depleted lakes

Filling up holes and craters
Creating reservoirs, its nature's
Way of self-preservation
Maybe it's time for reflection

There will be a time
Don't miss the sign
When the pools of water
Attract new life and mortar

To re-build a greater habitat
You can be quite sure of that
If you apply positive thinking
Rather than feeling yourself sinking

It's a time for planting new seeds
Watering them all so it feeds
From your nurturing hands
Spreading wholesome vegetation across your lands
Reaping from your sadness
To spread about abundant gladness

Tortured love

Twisted turns
Rocky paths
Golden sands
Soaring eagles and then crash.

Broken flight, damaged wings
Heading southwards at 100 miles an hour
Into severed cliff edges
Caught unawares.

Passing of light

Do not weep for me
Or shed sorrow for my passing
Instead cry tears of ever-lasting memories
Of the times we shared

The smiles
The laughter
And the love
That embodies our souls

And unites us as one
Under the stars
Among the rainbows
And the guiding light

From the heavens above
For I am present
Always
In your heart

Whispering to you
In the wind
Guiding you with my steady touch
On your shoulder

Rest your weary head
My precious angel
Take shelter
In my protective arms

That showers you
With the radiance
Of my spirit
And then be still

In the silence
Hear me
I will hear you
And be your listening ear

Whenever you need me
I will continue
To be your voice
Of reason

For we are all light

Acceptance

———

Acceptance is the ability to deal with something, someone or a situation, which is often negative, in a positive way, without attempting to change the outcome.

It is when you decide not to take action or try to change something or someone, or an outcome. It is 'accepting' what is.

This level of self-awareness is a skill that is not easy to achieve. Without acceptance we might feel weighed down, immobilized or overwhelmed with thoughts of apparent injustice.

Sometimes we have to accept a sudden loss, a long-term or terminal illness, disability, redundancy, financial loss or the break up of a relationship or friendship. This can produce anger, upset, sadness, frustration, resentment and feelings of hopelessness and impotence.

In many respects, 21st century living has a lot to answer for. As a consequence of modern life, the majority of us are less tolerant and ultra-critical, as much with ourselves as with others. We are more impatient and quicker to reach boiling point, jump to the wrong conclusions and react where we ought not. Many relationships are suffering as a direct result.

We live in an era of instant gratification. We seek and have come to expect perfection. We want everything faster, whether in material things, in ourselves, in our work and colleagues and in our nearest and dearest.

This is not surprising given the pace of life today and the resources at our disposal. As a result, we are impatient with ourselves and others. We have become dismissive of anyone – including ourselves – that doesn't measure up to our self-imposed exacting standards.

Wouldn't it be wonderful to be able to allow yourself – and those you love, know, work with or hang out with – to just be?

We all have acceptance at our core.
The stuff of our complicated and
cluttered lives is just layer after layer
of experiences and reactions that
we have carefully laid on top. If we
think we have no choice and that this,
today, is how our lives must remain,
we are wrong.

Acceptance is healthy and it allows
change to happen naturally. To be
accepting we first have to find out
what it is about ourselves, others and
situations that we find 'unacceptable'.
Once we have explored this, we can
ask ourselves:

- Is it something we can change?
- Is it worth changing?
- Do we really need to be in
  control of this?
- Are our reactions over the top?

Most of us could further develop:

- Acceptance of ourselves
- Owning our temperament, characteristics, emotions, actions, limitations and physicality. This does not preclude adjusting and changing those things of which we are not proud, or which are unhelpful to us
- Acceptance of others, especially those closest to us. Acceptance of their temperament, characteristics, emotions, actions and physicality

Acceptance does not mean that we have to allow and condone anti-social or unacceptable and unhelpful behaviour towards us, or by us towards others. We need to learn that there are things we cannot change or are not meant to change, both in our lives and in the lives of people around us and often in ourselves.

This means not rucking against the unchangeable and inevitable. Paddling upstream in this way causes heartache and wasted energy. Acceptance does not mean being or becoming complacent. It means that there are certain things in everyone's lives that are facts, whether in our environment, the people in our lives, our temperament and our physical/psychological/emotional makeup.

With the development of your innate skills of 'acceptance', you will acquire the ability to accept change, be more accepting of others and, most important of all, quieten the self-critic and become accepting of yourself.

11.

lover's merriment

attracting love

———

I've found my perfect melody

Floating atom

I'm floating in space
Drifting until I interlace
With another atom
There are so many phantoms
I need to avoid
Find my freakazoid

Night befalls the galaxy
No, I'll prove it's not a fallacy
To search trillions of miles
Across the milky Niles
Riding the superhighway
Until I hear it say
Come hither, feel me twitter
You're shaking me up like a transmitter
Radius of lively energy
I've found my perfect melody

A rainbow of colours flash
Ferocious, passion, scatters a sash
As the two collide, connect us as one
Creates vast illusion brighter than the sun
An electrical current, transcends time
Like a mystical implosion, a velocity of shine

I want to dance in your eyes

I want to dance in your eyes
Drink you in
Satisfy my thirst
So that my cup overflows
With merriment, drunk
Feeling high
Floating in the sky

Where the heavens meet
Meet the horizon
Joining, complete, an infinite line
Line of unity, unbroken, forever

A protective border
Of the two worlds
Heaven and earth
Swimming in your ocean
Your eyes, window to your soul

Falling deeper and deeper
Uncovering your buried treasure
Becoming your tidal, sweeping
Swooshing, awakening the bed floor
Stirring, a force not to be reckoned with

Nature's way, unstoppable motion
Power, driving hitherto
But never drowning, rush, push
Forming life, whirring
Changing direction

Settling, smooth, calm waters
Drawing breath, regulating
Mystery, unchartered, here we go again
I want to dance in your eyes…

Pair of doves

Two lotus leaves
Tendrils sprouting
Into a fountain

As the water pours
Two doves soar
A tender kiss
Love defenceless
There are no boundaries

They fly above the trees
Away into the heaven
The skyline the colour of watermelon
Ruby, red, orange, yellow and green

It's all serene
Soul-mates
Destiny and fate

Attracting love

———

As teenagers, the majority of us have little or no self-esteem. We also have anxiety about our bodies and whether we will measure up to perceived expectations.

At this stage of life, we worry about our shape. We look at models in magazines and the media, and we feel we can never measure up. It's all about looks.

We are convinced that we will never be asked out, or have the courage to ask anyone out.

This is where it all begins – low self-esteem. Because every one of us is unique, we all react to those initial let downs and blows to our confidence in different ways.

Some have the ability to rise above it, while others crumble, want to hide in a shell, then finding it difficult to come out of that shell. These young people become ever more self-critical, lowering self-esteem even further.

So then comes the next phase of the dating game. You are asked out! Or, perhaps you've had the courage to ask someone out! Someone *actually* wants to go out with you! How can that be possible? Perhaps you're not that bad after all!

However, this relationship can either be the making or the breaking of you. If, for example, the person you're going out with is a bully – and this is usually because they feel inadequate and take pleasure in belittling you, it can be enormously damaging. When you go on to your next relationship, your only experience has been negative.

The tendency then when you meet someone else is to be attracted to a familiar energy, this person is emitting. More often than not we fall into the trap of being seduced by this familiar, though negative vibration or energy, which is sadly the same negative energy we encountered in the previous relationship.

This situation can be very repetitive until we become aware, either by an outside influence or through self-realisation and awareness that this is what's happening. It's now time to break the pattern.

It can be done. It's a learning curve, but it's doable.

There is a way to combat the repeating
pattern of disastrous relationships.
Meditation helps to grow and
reinforce our feelings of self-worth,
self-awareness and self-esteem.
Meditation is not a magic wand, but
it starts off the process of change
and strengthening within ourselves.
The more we practice, the more we
can effect this invaluable change.

With this new self-awareness, we will naturally look for something entirely different. We will learn not to run headlong into relationships. We will want to get to know someone before we place our emotional selves in their hands.

We will naturally want better for ourselves and understand that we deserve to be treated with respect. We will revert to the good old-fashioned way of dating, actually getting to know someone before we jump into bed and lose control of our emotions. Before you know it, you're in a relationship, and you don't really know that person.

You have to step back a bit, observe and get to know that person in different situations so that before you give your emotions away, you know who you are actually giving them to. You know if you can trust them. Does this mean your relationship will actually work out? No, but it gives you a much better chance.

I'm a great believer that we find the right person when we have learnt to 'stand alone', not be needy, and realise that the right partner for us will also be independent and balanced. When we can fully accept someone, warts and all, and still feel they are worth being with, unconditional love comes into play.

12.

loving
relationship

*unconditional
love*

———

hearth and home

Hearth and home

You are my hearth
And my home
And wherever I roam
You are present
Like a flower
You have power
You have seeds
That feeds
My soul

Guardian angel

You're my angel
And in your arms you cradle
Me, longingly and lovingly
It's so comfy

The feathers of your wings
Are made up of swords from a thousand kings
Knightly and gallantly, I feel immune
From life's suffering and woes
A shield of protection you offer
Wholesomeness from your endless coffer

To nurture and to help me grow
To comfort and to let me sow
My dreams and wishes
Feeding from your plentiful kisses

I am blessed with your presence
You're my first line of defence
Against the twists and turns of ills
You're my virtuous angel, you fill my gills

With the purity of air
In your arms you tenderly care
That allows me to share
My gift of love to the world

Raptures of a fair kiss

Your kiss
I miss
From afar
I can still see you radiant star

Shivers run through my body
Like a river of thermal steam
Warming me from tip to toe
I hear your whispers flow

Communicating silently with me
Feels me with glee
There's a golden hue
Between us two

There's a magical air
All the wonderments of a fair
The dazzle and awe
An excitement that's raw

Childish and delightful
Sunlight and song
You and I belong
We walk hand-in-hand
For eternity across all land

Unconditional love

———

In recent times in the Western world, we have witnessed the breakdown of family and community.

Marriage became dispensable and family life fragmented. Priorities changed beyond recognition and society didn't catch up with the need to make family life manageable for people who are working. In the UK this is still an issue, while in other Western countries such as those in Scandinavia, it is better managed.

Nowadays people are content to live together as partners without feeling the need to go through a marriage ceremony. Somewhere in the future, we have to find the middle road and take our life relationships more seriously.

In fact, we all need to be more considerate with respect to the people who share our lives.

Tropical rainforest: passage of rites

Explore the depths of your intelligent mind
Draw forth your energy, passion, raw instinct

Your mind is a tropical rainforest
A deep blue river

An interwoven tapestry of vibrant colours
Mostly green, drawing forth from the blue

For it's the lush greenery and foliage that feeds you
What you see

And the feeling of searching, diving
Exploring into the hidden depths of life's meaning
That drives you, inspires you

Powers you on in your quest
For the meaning of your true path
Feeding your soul

Your heart
Your mind
Go and nourish your soul.

Your gift?
You

A powerful, wholesome force
Deliver change

Your truth?
An endless heart of love

About Sonia Wynn-Jones

———

I've been a regular meditator for more than 30 years. This practice and daily ritual has stood me in good stead through thick and thin and has been the saviour of my inner peace, health, balance and wellbeing for nearly half my life.

In the summer of 2011, I had cause to reflect on my years of meditation in a deeply personal and unexpected way.

I teach my clients that meditation is a tool for life, and I was reminded of this following the horrific car crash, in which my youngest daughter had a near death experience, resulting from a tyre blow out on a Los Angeles highway, which catapulted her onto the opposite side of the highway and head on into fast moving traffic, resulting in her car being reduced to a pulp with her inside.

That flight to LA is one I will never forget. The minutes felt like hours and the hours felt like days. I have never meditated as hard as I did in the eye of this personal storm. I was rewarded for my faith by finding my daughter alive, her brain and spine spared injury inside a body that was otherwise shattered.

When in need of support and rebalancing, meditation is an invaluable tool for calming, strengthening and inducing greater insights. Following my own advice, I meditated multiple times on this longest of journeys. I know that when I arrived at my destination, I was in better personal shape because of it.

I needed to be strong for my daughter and as the days unfolded, the one thing I could rely on was my personal commitment to my meditations.

So, even in the eye of a storm that has the potential to be a tornado in our lives, hold on to the fact that emergency meditations are exactly what you need to strengthen and handle any situation you meet.

'Meditation, a tool for life'

———

Sonia Wynn-Jones, MBRCP

(Member of the British Register of Complementary Practitioners)

Founder, Peace of Mind Meditation and Intuitive Counselling Centre Gifted Meditation Teacher and Healer/Counsellor

http://peaceofmind-online.com

About Natalie Cooper

Before having my son in September 2013, I was a successful, award-winning investigative business journalist and editor. I've travelled the world interviewing entrepreneurs and mavericks and been invited to guest appear on BBC Radio 5 Live as a media expert.

I adopted an intuitive style of questioning very early on in my career as a journalist and feel fortunate to have met and interviewed many individuals – each intent on making the world a better place.

People who've inspired me along the way include entrepreneurs, CEOs, directors, small business owners, board-level executive coaches, charity founders, Michelin-starred chefs, Olympic champions and elite performance business coaches, through to philanthropists, spiritual healers and some of the world's leading business thinkers and visionaries.

After becoming a mother, I took a career break. This gave me the opportunity to devote time to my creative passions and reinvent my career path while juggling childcare.

Meditation and intuitive guidance

―――――

A few months after the arrival of my son, I was struggling to cope. Issues I felt I had dealt with years ago, resurfaced in a magnified way. I turned to Sonia again, as I had not seen her for a couple of years. I was in a tailspin and I wanted to get out of it.

Sonia was the only one I trusted who I knew would be able to help and support me in the right way. She has this incredible 'knowing', being able to read your energy level, and has the gift of pure insight into what is affecting you and why.

First time around seeing Sonia, I learnt to meditate but I admitted I had got out of the habit pretty quickly after I stopped seeing her. Back then, I felt I had reached a place of contentment and was happy within myself. I didn't fully realise or even understand that meditation is something we must build into our lives and use as an ongoing daily tool, if we want to keep a steady ship.

This time around with Sonia, I was ready and open to go on a journey that would take me to a much deeper level of self-awareness than I had ever encountered before. I really listened and accepted all the guidance that Sonia imparted to me.

I knew I had to commit to the daily practice of meditation if I truly wanted to grow, let go of everyone and everything that was holding me back and change direction.

After a painful separation from my partner, and with a young child to look after as a single mother, it was time to regain control of my life.

Every word Sonia has written in this book is the truth. I know, because I have experienced all her teachings first hand. She has made sense of my journey. She's helped me to understand that we cannot change what has been, but we can change our way forward.

Through meditating daily, I have transitioned into a new phase of life. I feel absolutely liberated and at peace within myself. I can handle and juggle a multitude of tasks by organising my time way more efficiently than ever before. Is my life perfect? No. But I do feel I have achieved a healthy balance juggling childcare, work and life. I am able to stand alone, with confidence, because I'm doing it.

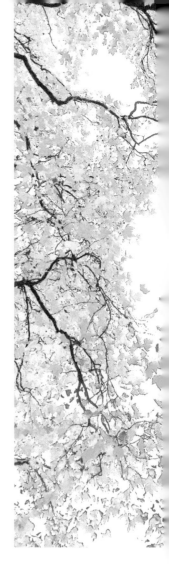

It takes incredible strength and courage to admit your own weaknesses first and foremost, to be able to forgive others and let go of fear, anxiety or insecurities. When you arrive at that place, you may still not have everything you want, but you do learn to accept what is and to be grateful for what you do have. I'm now following my true path and being true to who I am.

Meditation is something I have had to create space for, it was difficult at first, but I now know the impact it will have on my day if I do or I don't. Meditation sets me up for the day. There is a cause and effect. It is an inner sanctuary you can tap into, to give yourself time to pause, reflect, and calm your mind. Your intuition then comes into play and offers solutions, helps you problem solve and at times, temper your emotions if you need some time out, head space or some 'me' time.

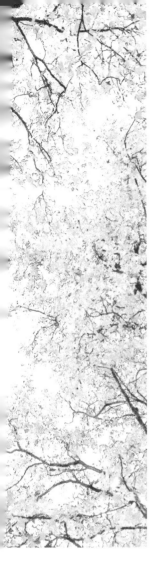

Development never stops. This is the most valuable lesson I have learned from Sonia. Even when you reach a stage of enlightenment, feel balanced and at peace, to maintain it, you have to keep nourishing yourself, to keep you straying off track when emotional triggers resurface when you least expect them. I am eternally grateful to Sonia for passing on her wisdom through her teaching.

Career transition

———

I've since transitioned into a visionary leadership and life balance coach. I now act as a guide to help people realise their vision and work through their goals.

I take an holistic approach, looking at all aspects of an individual's 'work', 'life', 'balance' because invariably they are all entwined.

My philosophy is if you can dream it and visualise it, you can achieve it.

The key is having the focus, clarity, and a clear vision. Through my coaching work, this is where I come in. Through asking questions, I take people on an inner adventure. A journey. To help them see, come up with choices and know what it is they truly want to manifest. Then, what it takes to bring that vision to life.

Coaching can be life-changing. By providing a very calm yet challenging space to help people reflect, explore and problem-solve helps them create solutions for a healthier way forward.

Follow your rainbow

___

When we learn to let go, we can realise our own gifts, talents and dreams.

We can find our way to a much happier way of life.

It's never too late to follow your dreams and change your way forward when you free yourself from the past.

We are all on our own individual journeys.

You are strong.

You have much to live for, to believe in yourself.

Love yourself for you.

Free yourself, find your wings, and fly, fly, fly, with grace.

With light,

Natalie

www.forest-whispers.co.uk

Guiding lights

——

I thank all of you who guided me
at poignant moments in my life.

To my dearest cousin Anthony Cooper,
and Ben Walton, your hearts are pure.

Thank you Di, Jules, Sue and Tola –
for all of your kindness.

Claire Morgan, Pips and 'uni' family,
Louise Scott, Yvonne Nelson, Rach,
Mel and Fern, I'm so thankful for your
generosity of spirit, love, and care.

And to great nanny Pauline, thank you
for all your support, protection and
words of wisdom.

Lastly, thank you to all my amazing
friends and everyone who has helped
me along the way, you know who you are.

You all gave me the courage to fly.

I'd like to say thank you to Stephen,
you've always been, and still are, my rock,
and to our adorable little boy, Finley.
We are so proud of you, always.

Authors:

———

• Natalie Cooper
www.forest-whispers.co.uk
forest_whispers_book

———

• Sonia Wynn-Jones
https://peaceofmind-online.com
peace_of_mind_meditation

Special mention to:

———

• Anna Green: cover & book design
www.siulendesign.com

———

• Cara & Cathryn Wynn-Jones: book trailer
Lodestar Author Services

———

• Darren Robson: founder & chairman
www.moefoundation.com

———

• Julia Ruppert: HCPC registered art therapist
https://collective-arts.org

———

• Berkeley Farm & Nursery
Lambourne End, Romford

Photo credits

———

- Page 39: Sonia Wynn-Jones

———

- Page 40: Amanda Richardson

———

- Page 178: Richmond Park
www.royalparks.org.uk/parks/richmond-park
(Please note, visitors to Richmond Park should be at least 50m away from deer for their own safety. This stag photo was taken with a zoom function on the camera).

———

- Page 181: Victoria Shillingford, Goddess Temple Gifts:
https://goddesstemplegifts.co.uk

———

- Pages 315, 319: Kew Gardens
www.kew.org

———

- Pages 357, 367: WWT London Wetland Centre
www.wwt.org.uk/wetland-centres/london

———

- Page 370: Statue of Liberty, Cara Wynn-Jones

———

- Pages 394, 399: East Sheen Allotments Society

Lightning Source UK Ltd.
Milton Keynes UK
UKHW050841030123
414526UK00002BA/38